Best Things In Life
Edited by Mark Richardson

First published in Great Britain in 2006 by:
Young Writers
Remus House
Coltsfoot Drive
Peterborough
PE2 9JX
Telephone: 01733 890066
Website: www.youngwriters.co.uk

All Rights Reserved

© *Copyright Contributors 2006*

SB ISBN 1 84602 697 0

Foreword

'My Favourite Things' poetry competition indeed captured the imaginations of young writers across the nation as we received thousands of poems about what made the authors smile, laugh, feel happy and joyful, whether it be a hobby, a pastime, an event, a person or something else.

We are proud to present *My Favourite Things - Best Things In Life*. So much thought, effort and creativity has been put into each and every poem cradled between these pages and we have enjoyed reading every single one. The task of selecting the overall winner was enjoyable, but nevertheless, a difficult task. You'll find the winner and runners-up at the front of this collection.

Young Writers was established in 1991 to promote poetry and creativity writing to school children and encourage them to read, write and enjoy it. Here at Young Writers we are sure you'll agree that this fantastic edition achieves our aim and celebrates today's wealth of young writer talent. We hope you and your family continue to enjoy *My Favourite Things - Best Things In Life* for many years to come and hopefully inspire others to put pen to paper.

Contents

Ambar Kerr-Wilson (11)	1
Amy Hawthorne (10)	2
Kitania Popple (9)	3
Anna-Leigh Brookes (10)	4
Katie Littlewood (9)	5
Rebecca Walsh (9)	6
Amelia White (9)	7
Sophie Spicer (10)	8
Samaira Farid (11)	9
Layna Youngman (9)	10
Dannielle Johnson (9)	11
Georgina Kerr (10)	12
Sophie Peacock (10)	13
Jessica Greatorex (10)	14
Melissa Canning (11)	15
Gemma Williams (10)	16
Eleanor Haughey (10)	17
Laura Thomas (10)	18
Jenny Baker (9)	19
Manpreet Rajbans (10)	20
Hazel Ijomah (11)	21
Sadie Bridger (11)	22
Daryl Holden (9)	23
Toni-Louise Ciplinski (11)	24
Emma Thomas (11)	25
Luke Smith (11)	26
Reece Martin (10) & Christopher Martin (12)	27
Ellie Edwards (9)	28
Amiee London (11)	29
Joshua McKenzie (11)	30
Hannah Edwards (9)	31
Lydia Blume (11)	32
Lucy Miller (12)	33
Rose Llewellyn (11)	34
Tiffany Hadman (9)	35
Megan Davey (10)	36
Susan King (11)	37
Charlotte Albiston (11)	38
Ryan Hunte-Christie (9)	39

Naomi Smart (10)	40
Leila Peck (9)	41
Bethany Stevens (8)	42
Joe Tetley (11)	43
Leah Green (9)	44
Jane Lerwill (11)	45
Kayley Maxwell (10)	46
Ethan Young (11)	47
Nicole Wermter (11)	48
Aoife Devine (11)	49
Alice Moore (9)	50
Scott Shannon (12)	51
Sanna Saleem (11)	52
Jodie Moore (10)	53
Fawzan Parkar (10)	54
Jessica Bacon (10)	55
Sophia Djerkallis (11)	56
Amy Baldwin (14)	57
Heather Deal (9)	58
Lucy Schofield (10)	59
Catherine Peach (12)	60
Bethan-Victoria Hartland (10)	61
Rebecca Graves (11)	62
Jamie Cooper (10)	63
Elrica Degirmen (10)	64
Emily Waters (11)	65
Shazul Islam (10)	66
Tanya Healy (10)	67
Rhianne Lounds (9)	68
Stephanie Wallace (10)	69
Megan Robertson (10)	70
Lauren Monger (10)	71
Christopher Wray (10)	72
Thomas James (11)	73
Stephanie McKeeman (10)	74
Elinor Hardcastle (9)	75
Aqsa Hussain (11)	76
Zora Owen (11)	77
Raymond Egualeonan (9)	78
Jennifer Ramsay (10)	79
Joshua Poole (13)	80
Maisie Hines (10)	81

Hannah Watson (9)	82
Ruth Mukonoweshuro (9)	83
Harriet Marchesi (10)	84
Suzy Hatton (7)	85
Emma Ibrox McLachlan (9)	86
Elly Lartey (8)	87
Daniel Godwin (10)	88
Abdurrahman Raqib (11)	89
Cara Loukes (11)	90
Parvinder Kaur (9)	91
Laura Baylis (10)	92
Poppy Gamble (10)	93
Ryan Lambert (10)	94
Aliya Yousaf (11)	95
Mutsa Chinembiri (9)	96
Charlotte Winterflood (12)	97
Nicole Ansell (12)	98
Jordan Nettley (9)	99
Omais Mazhar (9)	100
Rhia Walton (11)	101
Rebecca Pritchard (11)	102
Leighanna Levenie (9)	103
Jade Adams (10)	104
Kimberley Homer (11)	105
Callum Jordan (10)	106
Paris Maddock Dickinson (11)	107
Vicki Connelly (10)	108
Harry Harvey Wood (11)	109
Megan Wookey (9)	110
Chloe Taylor (10)	111
Annabel Bates (9)	112
Brook Vaughan-Eason (10)	113
Daniel Siddorn (11)	114
Natalie Summerscales (11)	115
Isabelle Smith (9)	116
Antonia Dore (10)	117
Kate Ramsay (10)	118
Alexis Dasiukevich (9)	119
Timothy Dasiukevich (11)	120
Katie John (9)	121
Annika Guru (8)	122
Sophie Garside (11)	123

Chloe Pendlebury (11)	124
Shyanne Duffus (10)	125
Hollie Smith (11)	126
Maria Tomaszko (9)	127
Katie Boekestein (7)	128
Lauren Vine (10)	129
Qudsiyah-Bano Agha-Shah (9)	130
Angel Panford (7)	131
Anisa Howell (11)	132
Bopski Mbadiwe (8)	133
Tehreem Sehar (10)	134
Zainab Darong (12)	135
Dylan Van Lengen (9)	136
Shazia Tahir (11)	137
Rianna Dathorne (11)	138
Michelle Bailey (15)	139
Lucy Macleod	140
Amy Robinson (11)	141
Charlie Emsley (13)	142
William Carey (9)	143
Heleana Neil (10)	144
Sapphire Walker (13)	145
Sian O'Loughlin (10)	146
Dominic Hughes (8)	147
Siddrah Shahid (14)	148
Natalie Steinmetz (12)	149
Amy Hodgkin (9)	150
Melissa Manrow (10)	151
Sophie Meyer (8)	152
Rachael Lyon (9)	153
Hannah Shore (8)	154
Atlanta Repetti (10)	155
Eve Richardson-Baldwin (9)	156
Danielle Elizabeth Bono Davies (11)	157

The Poems

Untitled

Playing the chanter and making coffee
Going to Braemar looking for squirrels
Playing with my little sister and having fun
These are a few of my favourite things

Looking forward to seeing everything
The smallest and largest creatures
The flowers blooming and birds singing
These are a few of my favourite things

When the hens cluck the chickens cheep
The cockerels crow, the ducks quack
The lambs bleat and the dogs bark
These are a few of my favourite things

Hearing my mum and dad call
Playing with my pets and other animals too
Going shopping and learning at school
These are a few of my favourite things

Sandi Thom and Westlife songs
Playing on my bike and go-kart
Smiling when I see my family
These are my favourite things.

Ambar Kerr-Wilson (11)

My Favourite Thing

My favourite thing consists of fun,
Chocolate melting in the sun,
I still eat it, I don't care,
Only because you are there.

You've made me ponder my favourite thing,
Is it to dance or to play or to sing?
It can't be true, it can't be right,
Only when you're in sight.

On my Nintendo,
Reading a book,
I can't enjoy these things,
But look.

There you are Ellis,
The wind in my wing,
And I can say
You are my favourite thing.

Amy Hawthorne (10)

Surfing

Surfing, the best feeling in the world
Free fall down the wave
I have to be brave
My heart is pumping
I am alive
This gives me the drive
To catch another wave
And again to be brave
Pumping the board to get more speed
On this one I am freed
From cleaning my room or walking the dog
And all those other boring jobs
I'm doing what I enjoy the best
I'm riding the crest
Drop off the back and paddle out for another
Watch the sunset while I wait
The horizon is beautiful, here comes a set
I catch another and tuck into the pocket
This has got to be as good as it gets
The next wave's here
I let out a cheer
I've been tubed!
I am at an all time high
Stoked!
Final wave for the day, I need my kip
Back up the face and hit the lip
Uh-oh!
Wipe out!
I surface with a grin
This is my favourite thing.

Kitania Popple (9)

My Favourite Things

My first favourite thing is gymnastics
Where I can do round-offs, nearly a back flick
My gym club is called Andover Springers
Where I am known as the Flying Winger
I run like a bullet, flying through the air
Preparing for a handspring that will end with a flair

My second favourite thing is trampolining
Where I jump up and down, landing with a ping!
I am on badge eight which is proving very hard
I really want to pass on Lynsey's tick card
Seat drops, front drops, easy for me
Front somersaults, back somersaults a bit more tricky

My third favourite thing is my cute Baby Born
I can dress her in anything, even school uniform
I have the ethnic, my sister has the white
No matter the colour we all have rights
When I go in the bath she comes in too
I always carry a spare nappy, in case of a poo!

My fourth favourite thing is going on shopping sprees
Spending the money that Mum says grows on trees!
Toys 'R' Us, Argos here I come
I look in these shops to find bundles of fun
When I arrive home I share out the things
I love to see all the happiness and laughter it brings

My fifth favourite thing is playing with my pet, family and friends
I love all the enjoyment and hope it never ends
We play lots of games like 'kerby' and 'tag'
We even put lots of make-up in our bag
This is my poem about my favourite things
I hope you enjoyed it and it would be great to win!

Anna-Leigh Brookes (10)

My Favourite Things!

My favourite things, I cannot explain,
For they are seven animals that I can't train.
I like other things as well,
Some things I like, I just can't tell.

Two friendly dogs and three little rats,
No one in our house is very fond of cats.
Count my two sisters as animals, they are unpleasant to say,
For they are horrible and vicious every day.

Lucky is my little white rat,
She's small and thin and isn't fat.
Berry is her annoying friend,
She bounces in my dressing gown, driving me round the bend.

Tessa is my funny brown dog,
She's mad and bouncy; she's even worse than a frog.
Pass her a ball quickly, she's running around being loony,
She's even faster than Wayne Rooney.

Zeus is a black nice dog, we never have to shout,
But poor old Zeus, he has some issues to work out.
He loves his dinner and loves to play,
My big boy Zeus, hooray! Hooray!

Peggy is a biting black rat, she bites me on the face,
She even bit me on my armpit; she's the rat I have to chase.

I like to play music; I play it mostly at school,
I want to play the saxophone; I think it's really cool.
I already play recorder and violin,
The bad thing about violin is that it really hurts your chin.

I love playing with toys,
Being a nuisance and making lots of noise.
Did I mention that I love reading SpongeBob,
I want to be a cook when I grow up; I haven't yet got a job.

Katie Littlewood (9)

My Friend Michelle

My friend Michelle is a lovely girl,
She lights up my life with one big twirl.
Even though she moved from my school,
I still think she's rather cool.
Nearly every day I go to her house,
But we are never quiet like a mouse.
Every day we have some fun,
When we're hungry we'll eat a bun.
We both like animals of every kind,
Even if they're old and blind.
Michelle's parents are from Hong Kong,
When she goes there the flight is long.
The food they eat is mostly rice,
We all think it's rather nice.

Rebecca Walsh (9)

Sleepovers

I go to my friend's house
And have a lot of fun,
Then we go shopping
And buy an iced bun.
Then we go home
And play a little game.
Then we sit quietly
And think of our fame.
Then it's time for bed
But no, no!
We sit up whispering
Putting on a secret show.
Then when we're finished
And have had a little rest,
We stuff our faces with chocolates
It's simply the best.

Amelia White (9)

The Holidays

The holidays are here
Don't worry about school
Forget the homework
No more books

The holidays are here
It's time to have fun
Go partying with my mates
And stay out late

The holidays are here
Let's have a great time
All come round
And play some games

The holidays are here
Let's catch TV
And eat ice cream
Or maybe some sweets

The holidays have ended
It's back to school
No more fun
But instead there's homework.

Sophie Spicer (10)

My Hobbies

Rounders and cricket
A cinema ticket
Football and hockey
Sweeties and choccie
English and art
A fresh new start
All of these thing are too good to be true
Cute dogs with tails
And my twinkling nails
Loud feathery parrots
Horrible, crunchy carrots
Sharp little claws
Cute soft paws
All of these things are too good to be true
Adorable, smiley faces
In small crowded places
Designer clothes
Sparkling toes
Cartwheels and handstands
Go England
These are all of my favourite things.

Samaira Farid (11)

My Favourite Things

Summertime is the time to be out
With my friends we play about
Dancing to my music, it makes me sing
These are a few of my favourite things
Putting my feet up and watching a movie
This I find is really groovy
Chatting to my friends when the phone rings
These are a few of my favourite things
Going swimming and acting the fool
This certainly is my biggest rule
Catching butterflies with beautiful wings
These are a few of my favourite things
Eating ice cream and plenty of sweets
I love to have lots of treats
History at school, learning about queens and kings
These are a few of my favourite things.

Layna Youngman (9)

Hugs Off Mum

I like going to the beach
Playing in the sun
But best I like hugs off Mum.

I like feeding ducks at the pond
And pretending I'm a shark
But when I get scared I run for a hug off Mum.

I like ice cream, I like fish
I love my mum's sweet kisses.

I like riding my bike,
I really like to hurry
But when I fall off I like hugs off Mummy.

I like going to the theme park
And trying all the rides
I like to hide especially with Mum.

I like going on holiday, playing in the sun
Also I like swimming with my mum
I find it really fun.

I like Christmas dinner
It really fills my tummy
But most of all I like hugs off Mummy.

Dannielle Johnson (9)

Horse Riding And More

My most favourite thing is to ride
To ride along the tide,
On my most favourite horse named Polo,
But most of all I love to ride solo.

I like to ski
And I love to swim in the sea,
Soaring down the mountain top,
Feeling like you cannot stop.

I like to watch TV and read,
I like to plait my hair in a bead,
I love to bounce on my trampoline,
I also like to act in acting scenes.

Prezzies, sweets and treats,
Sucking lollipops and eating sweets,
Mum and Dad and my siblings too,
Sticking stuff, glitter and glue.

Wishes and dreams,
The moon and sunbeams,
All the queens and kings,
These are a few of my favourite things.

Georgina Kerr (10)

My Favourite Things

Football and acting
Playing in the garden and eating ice cream
Reading a book and letting out a scream
Relaxing on the sun lounger and chilling with my friends
Eating lots of sweets and receiving fantastic treats
Dressing up as a fairy and being very scary
Playing with my brother and getting hugs from my mother
Going for walks and having long talks
Those are my favourite things
Going to the beach and amusing myself with my Game Boy Advance
It's very cool would you like to take a glance?
Oh, and one last favourite thing is my family
These are my favourite things.

Sophie Peacock (10)

Fun And Games

Watching Blue Peter and doing gymnastics
Listening to 80's music, it's fantastic
Learning about history and Vikings
These are just some of my favourite things

Going on family days out and reading books
Family get-togethers and feeding the ducks
Making stuff out of cardboard and string
These are just some of my favourite things

Going on long walks and flying kites
Climbing trees and looking down on beautiful sights
Dressing up as witches and noble kings
These are just some of my favourite things.

Jessica Greatorex (10)

Things I Like

I love school and the swimming pool,
Bottle-nosed dolphins and the kangaroo,
One is brown and the other is blue.

Other animals I like are the cheetah and the horse,
One runs fast and the other runs a course,
I love to sing and shout with my brother,
But sometimes it does annoy my mother.

I like other things like toys and rings,
But like Maria sings, these are a few of our favourite things.

Melissa Canning (11)

My Favourite Things

I want to be famous, but not in this way
I want to be a poet one day
My poem will be about my favourite things
The first verse will be about diamond rings.

Diamonds sparkle, diamonds shine
I think diamonds are divine
They are on crowns, they are on rings
This is only the start of my favourite things.

I like the programme called 'Smart'
I watch it because it's full of art
I have so much fun at Hallowe'en
I love the pop star Avril Lavigne.

I love being parts in drama
And chocolate is a real charmer
Out of clothes, skirts are the best
But jeans really beat the rest.

Playing out and watching TV too
These are some of the things I like to do
I love drawing in my sketchpad
But above all, I'm football mad.

But my favourite thing
As well as football is to sing
So write a poem just like me
So now you have the lock and key.

Gemma Williams (10)

My Favourite Things

My favourite things, oh there's so much to choose,
Maybe it depends on my kind of moods.

Well, I like a stroll in the park,
Even when it's dark.
I like sports day at school,
Because I think it's cool.

I like an iced-bun,
Especially in the sun.
I like eating sweets
And those tasty treats.

I like to play with friends
Because the fun never ends.
I like to be with my sister, dad and mum
And I love it when my cousins come.

I like birthdays with a great big cake,
The cake which I help to make.
I like Christmas with a big Christmas tree
And lots of great presents, just for me.

Eleanor Haughey (10)

What Is My Favourite Thing?
(Dedicated to Ben Thompson)

Yummy chocolates, delicious to eat, are they my favourite thing?
Or scrumptious sweets for a treat, are they my favourite thing?

Or holidays in places that are far away,
Or a wonderful Christmas and a happy birthday,
Are they my favourite things?

Or cold snow in the winter and flowers in the spring,
Or all the prowling cats and pretty birds that sing,
Are they my favourite things?

Or watching TV and simply just having a rest,
Or always being busy and trying my best,
Are they my favourite things?

Or my loyal pets, wonderful family and fabulous friends,
Yes! They're my favourite things.

Laura Thomas (10)

Rhyming Favourites

Stars and kittens
Milkshakes and mittens
These are a few of my favourite things

Rabbits and parrots
Cupcakes and carrots
These are a few of my favourite things

A trip to the zoo
And reading books too
These are a few of my favourite things

Dressing up, nice and pretty
Telling jokes that are witty
These are a few of my favourite things

Playing with pets
Doing shrimping with nets
These are a few of my favourite things

Sewing with thread
Waking up in my bed
These are a few of my favourite things.

Jenny Baker (9)

Things I Love

I love beans and mash
Because they make me smash.
I love wearing jeans
With my best high heels.
I love dancing
With a bit of prancing,
I love singing
Along with springing.
I love PlayStation 2 games and playing in the bright sun,
Visiting friends at parties or holidays, great fun.
I love Hilary Duff,
Because she is buff.
I love reading books
But make sure it has good looks.
I love the TV serial 'Friends',
It is so funny yet so touching hope it never ends.
I love R 'n' B, hip hop
Because it makes me flip-flop.
I love my mum and dad
Because we love each other like mad,
I'd love to go to central London,
As it's my favourite destination.
I love it when Girls Aloud and McFly sing
Because they have a style to do their things.
I love occasions when I get presents and treats
Because I get to eat ice cream and sweets,
I'd love to have a little pet
And see it score a goal in the net,
So this is the end,
Of my favourite brand!

Manpreet Rajbans (10)

A Walk In A Park

A walk in a park is what I take
With an armful of brownies, biscuits and cake
I'll find a quiet corner to sit
As I remember my favourite things bit by bit.

Chocolate and sherbet and vanilla milkshake
Packing my bags for a day at the lake
Reading a book about pigs that could talk
And taking my dog for a lovely long walk
Listening to my Ipod, playing on my PSP
Having my cousins come round for tea
Meeting with friends to have some fun
And listening to my teacher tell an awful pun
Netball, hockey, athletics and swimming
Listening to the birds' wonderful singing
Lying on the beach and getting a tan
Hearing the tinkle of the ice cream van
Watching a movie or my favourite cartoon
Learning about the sun and the moon
Going to Thorpe Park to enjoy the rides
Going to the seaside to watch the tides
Solving a hard logic puzzle with ease
Winning a chess match with casual expertise
Viewing the beautiful sun go down
And having a ride on the merry-go-round

A walk in a park is what I take
With an armful of brownies, biscuits and cake
I'll find a quiet corner to sit
As I remember my favourite things bit by bit.

Hazel Ijomah (11)

What Are My Favourite Things?

Writing stories are so much fun
Swimming and bike rides in the sun
Sleepovers with friends, meeting new people
These are a few of my favourite things.

Making stuff is so much fun, I could do it all day long
Playing on the computer, making up a song
Sewing lavender pillows, knitting a chair cover
These are a few more of my favourite things.

Playing on my Nintendo games
Cuddling the kittens and giving them names
Walking my dog is also a favourite
These are a few of my favourite things.

Playing the PlayStation with a neighbour
Riding down the village doing Mum a favour
Another favourite is my grandad's cooking
These are more of my favourite things.

Getting dressed up for a big occasion
Packing my bag for a wonderful vacation
Making cakes with my nan is lovely
These are all my favourite things.

Sadie Bridger (11)

School Summer Holidays

Long lazy days to fill with fun,
A trip away in the summer sun.
Eating ice cream to keep me cool,
Or having a splash in a swimming pool.
A day at the beach is really good,
Having a picnic with lots of nice food.
Searching the rock pools for starfish and crabs
And getting my feet all covered in sand.

Daryl Holden (9)

Those Are A Few Of My Favourite Things

Camping in Cornwall and going to Brocklands
Playing in ball pools, slides and bouncy castles
Going to parties and having fun
Those are a few of my favourite things.

Going to the beach, having ice cream
Playing in sand, sea and sun
Shopping and buying lots of new clothes
Those are a few of my favourite things.

Being inventive and building too
Making stuff out of wood and string
Reading books and playing games
Those are a few of my favourite things.

Playing with bears and on the Game Boy
Doing gymnastics and winning awards
Brushing my hair and doing mad styles
Those are a few of my favourite things.

Reading magazines and listening to music
Messing my room and never tidying it
Playing in the garden, ruining the grass
Those are a few of my favourite things.

Toni-Louise Ciplinski (11)

What Are My Favourite Things?

My name is Emma
I've got to write what I like best
But that's a dilemma
I thought it'd be easy, ha - it's the hardest test.

I'll just have to choose
What I like and then I'll write
There's nothing to lose
So let's get down to business, alright?

I like to play
Especially with my friends
And I love May
Cos when it's sunny the fun never ends.

Harry would come next
Harry, who you say? Why Potter of course
It's all in the text
And the author made more magic than doors.

I like to speak Spanish
Cómo estás? (How are you?)
The answer is
Bien gracias, y tú?

Now I'll say goodbye
Adios, chau, whatever they say
But I must not lie
This poem was easy, though it took me all day.

Emma Thomas (11)

Untitled

The first snowflake of winter
The shining of glitter,
When Homer Simpson slouches,
When James Bond crouches,
Rappers wearing some bling,
Those are a few of my favourite things.

When the don gets shot,
In snooker when I pot,
When I start to draw,
When Arsenal scores,
Birds, eagles with feathered wings,
Those are a few of my favourite things.

Maths, science, literacy as well,
In Year 1 I learnt to spell,
Trips, treats, outings too,
Learn new things that I thought weren't true,
Prince, princesses, queens and kings,
Those are a few of my favourite things.

Luke Smith (11)

Four Seasons Of Our Favourite Things

I like cars that go really fast, the windows wide open, the wind
blowing my hair
Ice cream that melts down the cone onto my hand on a summer's day
Lying on my back in the garden watching cloud shapes float by
Splashing in a pool, spraying and soaking everyone in sight
Lying on the beach with my toes skimming the waves in the evening.

I love bright leaf colours in the park, on a grey, dull, wet day
Crackling bonfires and exploding fireworks on a dark, cold night
Fallen conkers and nuts returning to the trees with hibernating animals
Stocking up on my favourite trick or treat sweets and dressing up
for Hallowe'en
Jumping in piles of leaves and scattering them everywhere again.

Snowball fights with groups of friends, dodging and throwing
them back
Wrapping up warm and Christmas shopping
The heat from the McDonald's thaws my frozen fingers
Tinsel and bright decorations and children waiting to see Santa
Footprints in the snow and bright, warm looking clothes
Dreaming of mugs of hot chocolate and warm, cosy beds.

Spring lambs in fields of grass, baby bunnies on grass verges
Squirrels waking up from their long hibernation
Picking flowers for Mum and seeing her eyes light up
Buds appearing on trees, flowers of all colours, shapes and sizes
Eating Easter eggs with goodies inside, the smell of rain on fresh
cut grass in the air.

I don't have a favourite season but I do enjoy all those things.

Reece Martin (10) & Christopher Martin (12)

My Favourite Things

Going to the beach on a hot summer's day
Picnics and swimming and playing away
Playing in the park until it gets dark
Going higher than high on those things called swings
These are a few of my favourite things.
Going on holiday to somewhere that's hot
You'll never catch us in a place that's not,
Trying out lots of new foreign dishes,
Snorkelling in blue seas with lots of colourful fishes,
Coming home to sleep in my own bed,
Memories from the holiday fill my head,
Like the man with fingers full of rings,
These are a few of my favourite things.
Christmas and birthdays and a special dinner,
I know when Mum cooks I'll never get thinner,
Crackers, fairy lights and a big Christmas tree,
These are a few things that are special to me.

Ellie Edwards (9)

My Favourite Things

I like to eat veggies and meat
I like to play on a hot day
With a doll in a pram
Lovely teddies, a cuddly lamb.

I do so like to cook
I love to read my favourite book
I like to colour very neat
Then relax and put up my feet.

I like to play a board game
Then I get that feeling to complain
For pudding I like ice cream
In all the flavours you've ever seen.

When I just cannot sleep
I stare at the ceiling and count the sheep
I do dancing for a show
I do ballet wherever I go.

I like to do things right
I like my teddy with me at night
I'm always ready for what a day brings
As these are all of my favourite things.

Amiee London (11)

My Favourite Things

The beginning of summer, no more school
Hanging out with my mates, we think we look cool
Going on holiday - blue sea and sun
Lots to look forward to, we'll have such fun
Hamburgers, hot dogs, KFC too
Trips to the cinema, aquarium and zoo
Watching my favourite team play in a match
Well done Pepe, what a good catch!
Football and rugby, cricket and gym
Splashing in the pool, learning to swim
Scoring a winning goal in extra time
Now I can claim that victory is mine
PlayStation Portable, MP3, DVDs
Climbing over rocks and scaling tall trees
Snowflakes in winter on the tip of my nose
It looks just like Rudolph's
The way that it glows!
Hanging up my stocking on Christmas Eve
Wondering what treats Father Christmas will leave
Cute little kittens with sandpaper tongues
Cuddly puppies with round podgy tums
Daffodils, crocuses, baby lambs in the fields
First finding their feet, then kicking their heels
Chocolate eggs, eggs with shells that release fluffy chicks
To sit on my palm and make tiny tweets
Cuckoos in the wood announcing that it's spring
Blackbird and thrush - chests swelling as they sing
The promise and the joy these little creatures bring
These are just a few of my favourite things.

Joshua McKenzie (11)

Do You Like These Things?

Swimming outside and skipping in the sun
Going to school is good fun
Roller skating round in rings
Do you like these things?

Going on holiday is great fun
Eating ice cream has to be done
Listening when a bird sings
Do you like these things?

Playing football and bat and ball
Dancing at a disco in the hall
Watching fairies' wings
Do you like these things?

Watching a movie on DVD
While eating popcorn in front of the TV
Playing table tennis when the ball pings
Do you like these things?

Opening presents on Christmas Day
With toys inside for me to play
One is a puppet with strings
Do you like these things?

Hannah Edwards (9)

What I Like To Do

Playing in the park with all my friends
Going on all the slides that have massive bends
Having some fun and eating ice lollies
Going out shopping and choosing the trollies.

Buying new gifts with my mum and dad
Finding new friends, a girl and a lad
Painting a picture of my mum's front yard
And a little something for my sister's birthday card.

Picking some flowers from the newly cut grass
Watching my grandad go zoomingly fast
Computers and programmes and a fabulous game
Watching the pop stars getting all the fame.

I've told you all my favourite things
From flowers to birds that have wings
Now I'm going to play in the park
Until the sun goes down and it gets dark.

Lydia Blume (11)

Summer Life

Swimming with my family, bowling with my friends
Writing lots of poetry, the fun never ends.

Throwing parties, eating sweets, getting presents and treats
Looking forward to Christmas with a stocking on your bed
Or having your birthday with loads of presents instead.

Reading loads of books, writing loads of stories
Packing your suitcase ready for a holiday
Moving house or moving countries, cities or streets.

Eating an ice cream, licking a lolly, sunbathing in the garden
Having a peaceful walk with the birds in the sky
And the ladybirds crawling in the grass with the beetles.

Swimming with my family, bowling with my friends
Writing lots of poetry, the fun never ends.

Lucy Miller (12)

Things I Love

I love to go and camp
but not when it's damp
I prefer to go when it's sunny
cos it makes me feel funny.

I love to pull funny faces
and go to different places
France, Italy and the mountains
but best of all I love chocolate fountains.

I love to eat chips
cos I use my lips
I don't like them with pepper
cos they make me cough and splutter.

I love to ride my pony
but not when I'm lonely
I leave the saddle in the sun
and then I burn my bum.

I love to eat ice cream
but it makes me feel mean
when I don't have enough to share
it makes me stop and stare.

I love to ride my bike
and stop to watch the pike
swimming around in the lake
and I love to bake a chocolate cake.

Rose Llewellyn (11)

Most Favourite

I love birthdays the most
I love Christmas too
My favourite dinner is Sunday roast
My favourite colour is blue
I love going on holiday
These things make me glad
Most of all I like to play
With my most favourite mum and dad.

Tiffany Hadman (9)

My Favourite Things

Handstands and headstands and jumping around
When I get tired I'll collapse on the ground
Staggering up steep mountains till I reach the top
When I get there my ears go *pop!*

Swimming and swimming till I shrivel up like a prune
Waking up and reading 'Treasure Island' in my room
Staying in bed till 8.30 in the morning
Getting out my pens and doing some drawing.

Going out to town with my friends
Talking to my mum till I drive her round the bend
Singing to Hilary Duff in my home
Using my hairbrush as a microphone.

Playing Pokémon on my Game Boy
Doing Twister and playing with other toys
Covering my ears when my sister sings
These are a few of my favourite things.

Megan Davey (10)

My Pleasures!

Before I begin to tell you what I like to do,
I'll ask you to sit down with a cuppa or two,
Then take out this poem and read about me,
Because these are some things I do when I'm free.

I like to take my dog to the river to swim,
Because she likes to get wet and soak us to the skin,
She eagerly waits for the stick to be thrown,
Then she'll swim off to fetch it never wanting to go home.

Then when I get home I'll check on my pets,
I have three more you haven't yet met,
They are Silvia and Alfred, my two goldfish
And Speckle my calf who is a bit devilish.

When all is done and it is night,
I'll go to bed and switch on my light,
Then I'll take out a book and read for some time,
Before falling asleep and ending this rhyme.

Susan King (11)

Hear About My Favourite Things

Maybe I like seeing my friends
Well it really depends
If they're in a good mood or bad
Maybe funny or mad
That's one of my favourite things
I love to see my pony
Otherwise I will get lonely
I see her nearly every day
She also eats lots of hay
That's one of my favourite things
For my sports I love to swim
My coach is called Tim
We always do a stamina test
I always will try my best
That's one of my favourite things
I love to go on holiday
We went to Disneyland last May
I love to feel the golden sand
Sitting on my hand
That's one of my favourite things
I have many more favourite things
Another is to play on swings
To see my mum
To see my dad
These are all my favourite things.

Charlotte Albiston (11)

My Favourite Things

My favourite things I like to do,
Range from playing on my computer with friends,
To completing homework too.

I enjoy riding my bike up and down the streets,
Pretending I'm in a race, eager to compete.

Football is my best; I actually play for a team,
Battersea FC we're called,
We are the best, you'll agree.

Another favourite pastime is bowling, swimming
And going to the cinema,
Sometimes I have so much to do,
I forget to eat my dinner.

Rock climbing, tennis, skateboarding too,
Helping my mum around the house,
Must award me with a trip to Chessington Zoo.

Eating out at Pizza Hut, cooking with my aunt,
A little gardening here and there helps me to express my art.

Oh, there's so much I like to do, it's all so hard to describe,
But with the help from my mum to write this poem,
Hopefully I have won the top prize.

Ryan Hunte-Christie (9)

Germs

Red ones,
Blue ones,
Green ones,
Orange ones,
Even gold and silver ones.
Big ones,
Small ones,
Fat ones,
Thin ones,
And they're all in my mouth . . .
I like the red ones . . .
Which ones do you like?

Naomi Smart (10)

Summer And Winter

Summer

Playing on the beach and eating ice creams
Having a sleep, dreaming sweet dreams
Catching butterflies with beautiful wings
These are a few of my favourite things.

Winter

Opening presents at Christmas time
Writing poems that don't have to rhyme
Hanging up stockings with pretty gold strings
These are a few of my favourite things.

Leila Peck (9)

My Favourite Things

My favourite animals are
hogs and cats
also dogs to pat.

My favourite food is
strawberries and cream
topped with blackberries and chocolate dream.

My favourite toys are
books and puzzles
and the Barbie looks are at the double.

My favourite places are
home and the park
I dream of Rome on the Cutty Sark.

But most of all my favourite thing is
jumping in muddy puddles and settling down at night
as well as giving and receiving cuddles
before turning off the light.

Bethany Stevens (8)

Cricket

C atch
R un
I nnings
C aptain
K it
E ngland
T eam

I love it!

Joe Tetley (11)

What I Like About The World

The sun when it shivers among the summer sea,
All of us together, my friends and me.
Lying on the beach at night where you can see the moon,
Watching movies with camels trotting on the dunes.
Roses growing in flowerpots,
Beautiful dresses with lots of dots.
Just like the day, this poem is gone,
So with a swish of a tail and a blink of an eye,
This poem must now fly.

Leah Green (9)

Untitled

This is my poem so please don't go away
These are my favourite things that happened today
I was playing outside in the sun
When suddenly I started to run
My sister asked if I wanted some fun
So she pulled out a toy gun
But over Christmas I was going to my friends
We left we went round a lot of bends
When we were there we played lots of games
And gave each other different nicknames
We went outside and did different activities
Then we ate milk chocolate McVities
I then looked round the house at the different places
After that we pulled silly faces
Her brother went to play with his toy cars
So we went and stole his Mars bars
We went to her room and played with some dolls
We got out their tea set and gave them some bowls
We then put away all her toys
And went outside to see some fit boys
Her parents bought me a bag of sweets
And lots of other gorgeous treats
It's Christmas day, I have lots of presents
The table's laid, there's lots of pleasants
This is the best Christmas day
I got a horse, it eats hay
They're all finished, those Christmas days
I watched the firework displays
Now I am going home
Me, my pencil and my dog with his bone.

Jane Lerwill (11)

My Favourite Things!

Swimming in the ocean with the bright yellow sun
Eating ice cream and chocolate and having loads of fun
Wrapping up presents then tying them with string
These are just some of my favourite things.

Birthdays and Christmas, presents and cakes
Going to school and meeting my mates
Picking flowers when it comes to spring
These are just some of my favourite things.

Drawing and colouring, doing some art
Stitching and sewing, making some crafts
Watching birds fly and moving their wings
These are just some of my favourite things.

Smiling and laughing, playing with my brother
Going to sleep all snug under my cover
Waiting for my friend when the doorbell goes ding
These are just some of my favourite things.

A kiss from my mum and a kiss from my dad
Winning a gold, which makes me so glad
Skiing and bowling, learning to sing
These are just a few of my favourite things.

Kayley Maxwell (10)

My Golden Rule

Books to read,
Games to play,
Films to watch,
My ideal day.

Granpa and Nan,
My sister and brother,
My ideal world,
Wouldn't wish for another.

Talking to Mam,
Learning new things,
Lying in bed,
The joy it all brings.

Off with my uncle,
Out in the car,
Where are we going?
Don't care how far.

Playing with my cats,
Giving them food,
Hearing them purr,
Puts me in a good mood.

Meeting my friends,
Going to school,
Enjoy my life,
That's my golden rule.

Ethan Young (11)

My Pet Rabbit

Felix is a lovely bunny:
Sometimes he is very funny
He is my favourite pet
He laps the garden like a jet
He likes to do what rabbits do
And can get bored without you
I play with him a lot
Sometimes he gets hot
He is black and white. Watch out!
He may bite.

Sometimes Felix is good
Sometimes Felix is bad
But I still like to give him treats
Otherwise he turns sad
Felix's hobbies are to play
And also to nibble on hay all day
He hops around in his hutch
He is known as a Dutch
He washes himself like a cat
And he doesn't like to sit on a doormat

Felix is five months today
That means his birthday is one month before May
I like him very much
Especially when he is out and about in his hutch
Felix means the world to me:
He is an angel that glides freely.

Nicole Wermter (11)

My Favourite Things In Life!

Reading Jacqueline Wilson books,
Roald Dahl's too,
Horror movies that scare me,
With ghosts that go boo!
Kittens, puppies, horses,
Any animal at all,
And all of the seasons
Summer, spring, winter and fall.
Going on my bike,
Feeling the wind hit my face as I go fast,
Playing and having fun with my friends,
Always having a blast!
Spending time with my family,
Having the best of times,
Listening to music
And when a song I know comes on,
I like to mime.
I like writing poems and stories,
And doing karate as well,
And going to car boot sales
Hoping that my things will sell.
Dancing, shopping and rapping
Are also some of my favourite things,
And I love all of my jewellery
Especially my necklaces and earrings.
And last but not least
I do have to say,
That I am grateful to God
For letting me do all of these things,
By making me special in my own way.

Aoife Devine (11)

My One Favourite Thing Is Maggie May

My Maggie May eats the hay
Off the truck and pushes her luck.
That's my Maggie May.

My Maggie May spends all day
In the sand, rolling around,
That's my Maggie May.

My Maggie May eats all day
All her hay and I love her more each day,
That's my Maggie May.

Alice Moore (9)

Untitled

I love swimming in the sea,
Everyone I like my friends and me.
It's great building huts
Even if you get scars and cuts.
I play footie night and day,
It is the only game to play.
I love beating my dad at pool,
It is great fun and cool.
I love watching Linfield the blues,
Eating chocolate cake and chews.
In the morning I love walking my dog,
I enjoy playing hide-and-seek in the fog.
I like watching sports and The Simpsons too,
I like feeding animals ones that buck and moo.
I love cycling my bike,
That is one of the best things I like.
I enjoy going on holiday in the sun,
It is warm and lots of fun.
I like it when I'm in the school footie team,
That is because I am very keen.
Watching the World Cup is great,
I watched them all with my mate.
I like eating ice cream on a hot day,
Maybe in July, August or May.
Playing on a trampoline is what I like to do,
I can do a front flip better than you.
I love catching something with my fishing line,
As long as it's a fish it will be fine.
I like shooting people with my pellet gun
And them shooting me is not such fun.

Scott Shannon (12)

My Favourite Things

Singing and dancing is so much fun
Singing all my favourite songs
Playing in the park all day long
Parties and birthdays are OK
The best of all is going on holidays.

It's good to have friends
They make you happy till your friendship ends
Skipping and jumping is so good
My other favourite thing is eating food

My favourite animal is the rabbit
Eating chocolate is my habit
Playing all my favourite games
I really like my first name

Some books to read
To take the lead

My family brings . . .
And that's all my favourite things!

Sanna Saleem (11)

What I Like To Do

Some of the things
I like to do
Are playing on swings
And going to the zoo

I like to swim
And ride my bike
I like to sing
And fly a kite

I have some pets
Which I adore
But they're always asleep
When I head out the door

I like my bed
All cosy and warm
I lay my head
And start to yawn

I close my eyes
And start to dream
Of all the nice things
Tomorrow brings . . .

Jodie Moore (10)

Family 'n' Friendship

Love from Mum and a kiss from Dad
A hug from friends and a smile from Aunt
Playing with friends puts a giggle on my face
Scoring a goal makes me feel proud
Doing funny things makes me feel like a clown
Doing cheeky things makes me feel big.

Fawzan Parkar (10)

My Favourite Things

It keeps me calm looking at tropical fish,
Eating chocolate from a football dish.
Watching my parrots spread their wings,
These are a few of my favourite things.

Cups of coffee with biscuits and cream,
Going on rides that make me scream.
Playing in the park and going high on the swings,
These are a few of my favourite things.

Doing the gardening and pulling up weeds,
Sowing all of my friends' seeds.
I really like my little rings,
These are a few of my favourite things.

Going on shopping sprees spending my money,
My mum and dad are ever so funny.
Learning about all the different kings,
These are a few of my favourite things.

Jessica Bacon (10)

I Love . . .

I love hanging out with my mates,
making fun of chavs, 'Innit tho Blates'
I love dancing, getting down to the groove
I love restaurants so I can bust my gut with food
I love to go on MSN chatting with my friends
I love to go in lush cars especially a Mercedes Benz
I love to go on bike rides, feel the breeze through my hair
I love the way I dress, I love my grey flares
I love to drive my quad bike zooming up and down,
people staring at me, they soon become a crowd
I love to climb trees on a sunny day high up in the sky,
watching the birds fly and play
I love my birthday, every year my dad gets drunk on a lot of beer
I love computers, I'm a computer freak
I love trick or treating and eating all the sweets
I love holidays in the sun, so much to do, so much fun
I love football; being in goal
I love my mum's new little foal
I love to sing and dance and act, it will soon be my career,
I'm sure of that
I love my friends to come round mine, it's lots of fun
and we have a wail of a time
I love sleepovers, staying up all night, telling spooky stories,
giving ourselves a fright
I love being cheeky to all of my teachers
I love cute little furry creatures
I love playing my Game Boy and my other Nintendo things
I love going to the park with mates and playing on the swings
I love writing stories for people to read, giving them laughs
or scares all for free!
I love to be creative quite a lot
I love to save the world from an evil plot
I love my sister, she's so much fun
I love my brother but he's 21
I love my mum and dad so much
I love my dogs, they're soft to the touch
so that was my poem I wrote for you
I hope you enjoyed it and I love it too!

Sophia Djerkallis (11)

My Favourite Things

I have many favourite things
I don't know where to start
But the things I treasure most
Are closer to my heart
Like the memories of laughter
And my childhood dreams
Of fairy tale castles
And faraway streams
Of holidays to Paris
And cities in the sun
Of taking all the photographs
To capture all the fun
Those once-in-a-lifetime moments
You shared with all your friends
Saying farewell
When another adventure ends
So although I love my books
My mum's credit card, my ring
My memories are my magic
Which is my favourite thing.

Amy Baldwin (14)

Untitled

What is your favourite thing?
Is it learning to dance or sing?
Is it listening to the radio,
Or is it something I don't know?

Is it . . .
Watching television,
Or is it putting make-up on?

Riding your bike?
Flying a kite?
Having a water fight,
Or pushing a table with all your might?

These are a few of my favourite things
Including drawing butterfly wings.

Heather Deal (9)

My Favourite Things

I have many favourite things to do
like going to the park or visiting the zoo
but the thing I like to do the most
is taking a walk along the coast

The seaside is my favourite place
I like the sun upon my face
I look for shells along the way
I wish that I could stay all day

The rock pools full of things to see
the things that live within the sea
like crabs and fish and things to eat
a place to splash with my two feet

To build a castle in the sand
my dad will always lend a hand
we built the biggest on the beach
we hope the waves will never reach

We run along the sunny shore
we run and run and then some more
we breathe in all the salty air
my cheeks so healthy, pink and fair

I love the sound of breaking waves
and searching in the dark damp caves
where crabs lay hiding under rocks
oh, I wish I hadn't worn my socks.

Lucy Schofield (10)

The Best Things In Life

Going to the cinema with my best mates,
going in town, trying on new things,
playing with my mouse in his little cute house,
taking the dog for a walk and clearing my thoughts,
washing my hair to think about what to wear.
These are some of my favourite things.

I turn my music up so I can wind my mum up!
Walking on my mum's back and treating her like a mat,
holidays are the best because then I get a rest,
my bedroom is a mess and it is the best.
These are some of my favourite things.

Catherine Peach (12)

Favourite Things

MSN and talking to my friends
Walking and cycling around bends
Going swimming
And slimming.

Going out with boys
Playing with toys
Reading a book
Getting round the hook.

A kiss from my mum and dad
Doing a memory book in a notepad
Watching The Pussycat Dolls sing 'Sticwitu'
Making a card out of card and glue.

Playing with my kitten and cat
Putting my cat in a pink frilly hat
Doing art and history
Sorting out a mystery.

Watching TV
Doing PE
Having pens
Chewing pens.

Spending money
Being funny
Having my alarm clock go bing, ding, ding, bing
Seeing butterflies fly with their beautiful wings
These are a few of my favourite things.

Bethan-Victoria Hartland (10)

Families

Families are loving
Families are caring
Families are lots of fun
Families are funny
Families are like good friends
Families are always there to share
I love my family . . .

Rebecca Graves (11)

Favourite Things

Are these a few of your favourite things?
Unicorns, monsters and dragons with wings,
Maybe you like some PC games
And call all your people different names.

These might be your favourite things,
Seeing some movies with fighting in rings,
You might like playing with dolls and stuff,
Or getting stuck in a policeman's handcuff.

Do you think these are my favourite things?
Football or books or Pink Panther rings,
DVDs on tele or playing with friends,
Driving round corners or hitting dead ends.

I'll tell you these are my favourite things,
Football and tele, and books about kings,
Friends and their bikes, their toys as well,
But most of all I like using hair gel.

These could be your favourite things,
Violins and drums or guitars with strings,
It could be a recorder or a cello,
Making some notes high and low.

Jamie Cooper (10)

My Treasured Things In The Morning

The fragrant smell
Of fresh, floral lemons in the mid-air
When the unfolding of the light
Comes in at the crack of dawn.

The liveliness of the early light-hearted bird
Which gracefully approaches a summery apricot tree
It gently begins to sing a high-spirited melody sweetly.

The petite primroses which blossom with beauty
Tries to unravel its peach delicate petal
It grows and grows
Until it can no longer grow anymore.

The sacred sun is our sister
The morning star, she flickers
So strong, so bright
Her celestial light shines over the Earth
And the heavens above.

Elrica Degirmen (10)

A Few Of My Favourite Things

Drama is one of my favourite things
You get to wear make-up
And act like you're king
Act like you're happy, act like you're sad
Act like you're good, act like you're bad.

Singing is one of my favourite things
You get to express
Wear cool clothes and bling
Sing remix, sing hip hop
Sing pink rock, sing pop.

Dancing is one of my favourite things
Jumping and clapping
Bending and swing
Let's break dance, let's street dance
Let's clog dance, let's bring.

But this is my most favourite thing
Listening to Green Day
And the way that they sing
'Letter Bomb', 'Basket Case', 'Hitchin' A Ride'
And I hope you have the 'Time Of Your Life'.

Emily Waters (11)

My Favourite Things

Playing PlayStation games is the best
Out of Xbox and all the rest,
Playing new games, it's great fun,
Not as good as the water pistol guns!

Playing with friends forms a strong bond,
Splashing each other with a little pond,
Playing with friends all day long,
At night, singing our favourite song.

A mum and a dad, you won't be sad,
Giving you things you wanted, of course, you will be mad,
Getting so much love,
Letting you join so many nice clubs.

Shazul Islam (10)

A Kiss From Dad And A Hug From My Mum

When I fall and graze my knee
A kiss from my dad makes it all go away
A hug from my mum
Is like fluffy white clouds above
That makes me feel safe and warm
So a kiss from my dad and a hug from my mum
Makes me feel very glad when I'm so sad
Because they're the best mum and dad I could ever have.

Tanya Healy (10)

Childhood

Sea and sand
Shells in the land
Swimming in the sea
And listening to great bands
Playing in the garden
Cycling out with friends
Writing to my penpals
And finding things to mend
Buying sweets and ice cream from the local shop
Annoying Mum and being chased by her mog
Playing in the summerhouse
Looking in the pond
Spending time with parents
And making a special bond
Waking in the morning
Listening to the birds
These are all my favourite things
The best things in the world.

Rhianne Lounds (9)

Summer Holidays

In the summer holidays
I like to have long races
At all different types of paces
Running, skipping and jogging too
Putting paper together with sticky bits of glue
Playing with my toys
Annoying lots of boys
Jumping all around
Then falling on the ground
Playing hide-and-seek
Trying not to peek
Playing on my trampoline
While my brother's being mean
By doing lots of wrestling moves
When I'm trying to do my dancing grooves
Summer holidays are so much fun
Especially when you're in the sun.

Stephanie Wallace (10)

Summer Holidays!

In summer I like trampolines, bouncing up and down,
eating fruity ice cream and spinning round and round.

Holidays and picnics, playing in the park, climbing on the climbing
frame, it's really quite a lark.

Journeys to the seaside, holidays and fun, bubblegum and candyfloss
and playing in the sun.

Skimming stones and paddling, getting very wet,
trying to catch a little fish escaping from my net.

Riding on my bicycle, on ground that's hard and soft,
I feel the wind behind me, I'm nearly taking off.

It's the last week of the holidays, the fun has nearly gone;
new shoes, haircuts, uniforms, it really won't be long.

The holidays are over, it's really been a ball,
Pack my bags, I'm out the door . . .
It's time to go to school.

Megan Robertson (10)

The Magic Of Life

How I love the whisper of the leaves as they rustle through the trees
The flow of running water bubbling down a winding stream
The dancing of the flowers casting shadows on the ground
The gentle movement of the clouds drifting by without a sound

How I love the cautious watch of the vixen as she feeds
                                      her hungry cubs
The pleasure of the hippo as it wallows in the mud
The grace of the giant eagle as it soars across the sky
The bristle of the squirrel's tail as it silently scurries by

How I love the warmth of the shining sun on a summer afternoon
The drama of the lightning as it flashes across the moon
The chill of the autumn breeze as it swirls around my knees
The pitter-patter of the raindrops as it deepens rivers and streams

How I love the boats sailing steadily to a land across the sea
The crunching of the pebbles as I comb a stretch of beach
The softness of the golden sand underneath my feet
The freshness of the salty sea to cool the blistering heat

How I love the magic of life.

Lauren Monger (10)

Computer Twit

I'm a wiz kid on computers or so I like to think,
I've broken it so many times it seems to cause a stink.
My teacher's hair has turned quite grey,
Because I fiddle in the icon tray.

I like to use a lot of ink,
It's being creative I like to think.
My dad is going round the bend,
As there is always something for him to mend.

One time I put the blame on Mum,
I felt quite bad for what I had done.
I got a brand new microphone,
I broke it and I felt alone, my poor old microphone.

Our scanner is not working, for it is really far too old,
I tried to do my best to fix it even though I was not told.
I download quite a bit from the net,
The only problem is my parents fret.

I got into control panel only to check things out,
Just like incy wincy climbing the waterspout.
When something goes wrong and breaks,
My dad feels like throwing it into the lake.

If fiddling on computers is my fate,
Who knows, one day I might be the next Bill Gates.

Christopher Wray (10)

My Favourite Things

My favourite things are playing in the sun,
Running round naked, oh what fun.
Playing in the garden, doing stupid things,
Climbing in the tree house, swinging on swings.
Playing in water, always getting wet,
Climbing out when I want, then playing with my pet.
Camping in the garden, getting out the tent,
Cooking breakfast on the stove with my best friend.
Going on holiday, visiting my friends, going to their house,
My day is at an end,
Everyone's happy, what great news,
Playing in the sun is my favourite thing to do.

Thomas James (11)

Untitled

Putting on make-up,
Doing my hair,
Eating chocolate,
Without a care.

Skipping in the playground,
Walking the dog,
Watching telly,
Flicking through a catalogue.

Jumping in puddles,
Running around the house,
Giggling with sisters,
I'm louder than a mouse.

Baking cakes,
Swimming in the sea,
Cuddling my teddy,
I'm happy to be me.

Making up dances,
Flying away on holiday,
Shopping in town,
Sleeping at the end of the day.

Stephanie McKeeman (10)

My Hobbies

Dancing, singing, counting at school,
Those are the things I think are cool.
Shouting, screaming, messing about,
These things are bad there is no doubt.

Jumping, hopping, running all day,
Did you guess that I love to play?
Reading, thinking, dreaming too,
These are the things I like to do.

Horse riding, swimming, playing the guitar,
Everyone knows I love these by far.
Playing on my Game Boy, the computer too,
I love to do these things all day through.

Cheerleading, rounders, playing football,
Climbing a ladder on top of the wall.
Sitting at home, thinking about kings,
These are a few of my favourite things.

Elinor Hardcastle (9)

My Favourite Things

'Prince of Persia' and fairy tales,
Most of the time I manicure my nails.
I jump up and down,
Laughing like a clown.

Christmas brings presents and sweets,
Birthdays are better cause there's loads of treats.
Celebrity shows, 'The X-Factor',
Are they trying to sing or become an actor?

Necklaces, bracelets and rings,
These are all my favourite things.
Glitter and decorations are so great,
All of these things I will never hate.

Aqsa Hussain (11)

My Favourite Things

I like to play
Outside with friends all day
In the summer it's fun
Rushing about in the sun
Riding my bike
And doing what I like
A champion swimmer
I would like to be
With an Olympic medal, Mum says we'll see
Teenage programmes on TV
'That's So Raven'
'Zak and Cody'
The Disney Channel and soaps
Without them I just couldn't cope

My favourite game is Monopoly
I am always nagging Mum to play
My mobile phone is really cool
To text my friends it's a handy tool
Using the computer is so much fun
Playing games, they go on and on
I love to play Bratz dolls with my friends
So much to do the fun never ends
Street dancing and hip hop
Make me feel on top
Gymnastics and running
They are my favourite fun things.

Jennifer Ramsay (10)

My Favourite Things

My favourite things
I'm easy to please
Mum and Dad
Sisters at a squeeze.

Chocolate chip cookies
Strawberry milkshakes
Grated cheese sandwiches
My own picnic I'll make.

Nintendo DS
Xbox for sure
Yu-gi-oh duelling
Room for anymore.

The PC's a winner
Watching DVDs too
MSN keeps me in touch
It's so easy to do.

My two dogs are mad
I've got a rabbit too
Seven fish in a tank
It's like living in a zoo.

Joshua Poole (13)

My Favourite Things

Some people call me a computer wiz kid
And at football I am great in mid
PlayStation and my Nintendo DS too
But some things I just don't have a clue.

Hanging with friends is great fun
Football and trampolines in the garden
Playing with my dog is fantastic
So is my whole family sharing a picnic.

Playscheme and shopping with my mum
All this beats boredom
Winkle picking with my dad
Watching him being chased by a crab.

Fighting with my brother
Pretending I am tougher
Sleepovers are a bonus
Possibilities are boundless.

Put all these things together
To make a great picture
But at the end of the day
There is nothing to say
My favourite thing is fun!

Maisie Hines (10)

My Favourite Things

I like art
And making a mess
I do loads of sewing
To make the cat's dress

I listen to glam rock
Queen and Sweet
The members of the band
I'd really wish to meet

I go every week
To visit my nan
We take DVDs
Such as 'Spider-Man'

Those were three
Of my special pleasures
I'll always do them
And keep them as treasures.

Hannah Watson (9)

My Favourite Things

I like playing in the sun
And helping my mum do the cooking.

It is easy to see
That it is fun to be
A person with favourite things.

I have a bike
It is not a trike
It's a bike with two wheels.

It is easy to see
It is fun to be
A person with favourite things.

I have a tamagotchi to play with
And at the end of my bed is where my toys live.

I like plain ice cream
But if I don't get one I will scream.

It is easy to see
It is fun to be
A person with favourite things.

Like me!

Ruth Mukonoweshuro (9)

My Favourite Things

My favourite thing is my cat,
Who sits upon my knee.
She's always purring when I stroke her
And constantly smiling at me.

My cat is very affectionate,
She's furry and cuddly.
She loves to lie in the sunshine,
But still she's smiling at me.

I'd hate it if my cat died,
I'd miss her very dearly.
But my cat has got all nine lives
And will always stay smiling at me.

Harriet Marchesi (10)

Untitled

When I see my rabbit hop
I let him play with the mop
When it's hot he jumps
But when it's cold he shivers
But I wish he was soft
When it's summer I see him tough
But when it's winter I see him bored
But everyday he's different, I wish he was the same
Sometimes he is hot, sometimes cold
Sometimes bored, sometimes tough
All sorts of different things
But most of all he is the coolest rabbit in the world.

Suzy Hatton (7)

My Favourite Things

Playing with my friends in the sun
We like to have lots and lots of fun
Opening presents, getting treats
I like to eat lots and lots of sweets
Playing with my toys and visiting the park
Me and my friends always have a lark
Reading books that are so cool
I love going to the swimming pool
I love card making with my mum
The time I spend with her is always fun
Playing football with my dad
We run about and go mad
These are my favourite things to do
Why don't you try them
You'll have fun too.

Emma Ibrox McLachlan (9)

My Favourite Things

I like to read, I like to write,
I like to play, I like to sing,
I like to do some funny things.

I like to play with my friends all day long,
Again we'll sing a cheerful song.

Riding my scooter or riding my bike,
Skipping on my jump stick,
Oh it's very fun.

Going on my computer, painting is very fun,
Looking at my baby pictures and drawing too,
But most of all I like . . .
Roller skating!

Elly Lartey (8)

Good Things/Bad Things

Here are the good things in my life
Transformers, Yu-gi-oh
Star Wars, computer games.

Runescape, Xbox
Water, food
Milk, TV.

Mum, presents
'McFly', 'Girls Aloud'
Sun, rain
Bikes, skateboards.

Bad things are . . .
Girly shops, bedtime
Cleaning my teeth
Not allowed a new toy
Clothes, my brother.

Cats, pasties
Tidying my room, seeing kisses
Boredom, school
House rules, fruit.

This is good
This is bad
This is me
This is my life.

Daniel Godwin (10)

Intelligence Tankas

Technology's cool
Lets us do a lot of things;
Microbe dissection,
Finding quite high prime numbers,
Possibly find aliens!

Science is arcane,
Loads of things to discover,
Explains Saturn's rings,
It is true and serious,
Science is the thing for me!

Reading's really fun,
Colfer, Dahl, Horowitz, West,
Penguin, Scholastic,
All publishers or authors,
It is oddly relaxing!

Abdurrahman Raqib (11)

From Butterflies To Antarctica

Pretty coloured butterflies,
Pink, orange, blue,
Wing-flapping dragonflies,
Many colours too.

Scented floral power,
Roses, lilies, lavender,
Not one sour,
What's your favourite flower?

Can you guess who?
Fish eating, ice sliding,
I'll give you one more clue,
Penguins!

These are just a few of my favourite things.

Cara Loukes (11)

Florida

F lorida is a nice place to go
L aughter and joy everywhere you go
O ver there you will have great fun.
R ide in the plane
I f you go you will like it
D ancing to the cool music
A nd you will have a wicked time.

Parvinder Kaur (9)

So Much To Do

I do not have a favourite thing
There's so many things I like
I do like riding on my bike
I do like going on a hike
I do like learning in my school
I don't hate anything at all
I do like singing in the choir
I don't make friends with any liars
I do like telly
I do like the TV programme 'Kelly'
I do like animals big and small
I especially think dogs are cool
I like the colour blue
I love the smell of clothes that are new
I like making stuff out of clay
My favourite month is May
My favourite animal is the tiger
I even like creepy-crawly spiders
I love reading
But the best thing is succeeding
I love shepherd's pie
I love dreaming I can fly
I love sweets
I love the one called Marshmallow Treat
I love holidays
I love to daze
I love the sun
I love to have fun
But my favourite thing
Is being a poet.

Laura Baylis (10)

My Favourite Things

A hug from my mum, a kiss from my dad
My brother's soft cheek as he brushes past
My mum's voice in the middle of the night when I call her
My dad's van coming home at night
Running through the fields with Daisy, my dog
The knock on the front door when my friends call
The warm fire in winter when I come home
Curling in my bed after my bath
The fresh air in the winter mornings
Autumn leaves falling and rustling
Collecting conkers in the park
Lying on the grass counting the stars
Getting ready for Santa the night before
Opening presents on Christmas morn
The trip I had to Center Parcs
The warm sun on my face
The school bell at the end of the day
Listening to my music when I get home
Playing my piano when it sounds right
Bouncing on my trampoline high above the ground
Making art from rubbish, sticking them with glue
Hummers, camper vans, Minis too
Oil from Dad's Mini when he revs up the path
Seeing my family when I've been away too long
Watching telly when there is nothing to do
Playing with the PlayStation
Tracy Beaker, Mr Bean too
The taste of Galaxy when it hits my tongue
But most of all friends and family
These are just a few of my favourite things.

Poppy Gamble (10)

My Favourite Pets

Rabbit and dog hide in the fog
Moggy and mice are cute and nice
Pets meet at the vets to discuss their health
My pets are my favourite things
My dog likes to stay
My rabbit sleeps in the hay
The cat and the mouse live in the house
My pets are stuck in their ways
My pets have fun all day
They enjoy when they play
They love me in every way
That is why my pets are my favourite things.

Ryan Lambert (10)

My Favourite Thing Is . . .

My favourite thing is to write
And be absolutely ever so polite.
My favourite thing is to play
And have a fantastic day.
My favourite thing is to learn
And let all my terrible fears burn.
My favourite thing is to plant flowers
And fly to colossal towers.
My favourite thing is to swing
And bling-bling.
My favourite thing is to swim
And turn a little slim.
My favourite thing is to go to Rome
Which feels so much like home.
What's your favourite thing?
My favourite thing is to paint
And watch someone faint.
My favourite thing is to drive
And stay alive.
My favourite thing is to look at sheep
And go to sleep.
My favourite thing is to cook
And read a book.
My favourite thing is to eat
And make wheat.
My favourite thing is to meet the Queen
And Mr Bean.
My favourite thing is to have a gnome
As wonderful as my own home.
What's your favourite thing?

Aliya Yousaf (11)

My Holiday Fun

Rings, rings, wonderful rings
Are these a few of my favourite things?
Watching TV, playing in the sun
Visiting my friends and having fun
Listening to a riddle
Playing 'piggy-in-the-middle'
Whistling a tune
And admiring the moon
Playing with my cat
Pretending to be fat
Going to car boot sales
Swimming and acting like whales
Playing with my sisters
Pretending they've got blisters
Playing with my favourite games
Calling my friends funny names
Eating juicy oranges, lovely and nice
Going out shopping, wondering what's the price
Listening to smashing CDs
And brushing off my cat's fleas
Making a huge mess
Giving my parents stress
Climbing up and down the stairs
And eating lovely chocolate eclairs
Staring out to space
Standing in one place
Going for a jog
Sitting on a log
Getting a Christmas present
In the shape of the moon's crescent.

Mutsa Chinembiri (9)

Handbags And Shoes

Handbags and shoes are totally cool,
They're really trendy and they really rule,
Every girl should have some,
It should be the law,
Then everyone will buy more, more, more!

Pink, purple, red and blue,
All these colours will suit you.
Find an outfit which will look fab,
Pick some shoes and a handbag.
Your outfit is complete now
Let's go, you'll be the star of the show.

So you're finally the star
See how shoes and bags are first aid for all girls.
They complete every outfit that's for sure,
So let's give them a round of applause.

See why they're my favourite things,
Got to buy more until I can't carry any more
And my hands are full, full, full!

Charlotte Winterflood (12)

The Sleepover Party

I love having parties to get money
And buying a new outfit for my party.

Plus getting out our dairies
And sharing girly gossip.

Also love sitting down and getting our magazines out
And checking the latest news
And doing all the competitions to win prizes.

Staying up late and watching videos and DVDs
Going to the fridge and munching all the food.

I love doing 21 dares, that's the best thing about parties
Putting on the music, blasting loud
And waking up all the neighbours
And putting on dressing-up clothes
Dancing to all wicked tunes especially to R 'n' B

The most surprising things
About parties is getting presents
Don't come to my party
Without a wonderful present!

Nicole Ansell (12)

Untitled

Listening to CDs, as loud as can be
A day at the cinema, my brother, my sister and me.
Playing Yu-gi-oh cards and beating my friends
A trip to the seaside where the sun never ends.

On holiday to a caravan thanks to Mum and Dad
Then ten pin bowling when the weather is bad.
Swimming, diving and splashing around
Until it's time to go homeward-bound.

At bedtime, I love a good book,
The latest Harry Potter is worth a look.
Then on the computer when I should be asleep
Playing games, oh no I'm in too deep.

Out on my bike with the wind in my hair
Racing my green machine, giving everyone a scare.
Bouncing on the trampoline is a wonderful thing
Jumping so high, it feels like I have wings.

Annoying my parents is what I like best
It's my age, I know, I'm just like the rest.
But who knows what tomorrow will bring?
Perhaps all these won't be my favourite things.

Jordan Nettley (9)

The Spirit Of Summer Holidays

H opping around the garden,
O blivious fun in the sun,
L icking ice lollies, the summer holidays have begun!
I ncredible days filled with treats,
D angerous feats in the scorching heat.
A dventurous moments with old friends and new,
Y *ippee* you think, no more work to do.
S oon they will come to an end, as the sun sets on an eternal trend.

Omais Mazhar (9)

Spring

The sun smiles kindly, giving out beams of light,
While clouds float freely, through clear blue sky,
Birds singing happily, the wind in their wings,
The young lamb skips in a field of green, the horse canters away,
Piglets scramble noisily as the farmer gives them food,
Mother hen clucks angrily, her chicks wander off,
The farmer hums softly, warm air on his cheeks,
Snowdrops are dying, spring has arrived,
We are welcomed with daffodils,
Holding proud yellow trumpets up high.

This is spring, it is my favourite thing.

Rhia Walton (11)

My Favourite Things

My favourite things are so cool
I really enjoy playing football
Playing out with my friends
I hope this fun never ends.

I also like playing on the computer
And riding on my electric scooter
Having a kiss from Mum and a hug with Dad
That's the most fun I've ever had.

Shopping for clothes
Painting my toes
Playing cards with my brother
And annoying my mother.

Going out and buying earrings
These are just a few of my favourite things
When I am older I hope I still have fun
Playing with my sister in the sun.

Rebecca Pritchard (11)

The Beach

Green, blue, salty sea,
golden-yellow shiny sand,
creepy crabs, sticky starfish,
melting ice poles in a cold winter breeze,
waving towels and wet sandy feet
see the clear blue sky while lying on the beach.

Leighanna Levenie (9)

Splits, Cartwheels And Headstands

I love doing cartwheels,
Round and round I go,
Head over heels, heels over head,
I think it's really fun,
I practice in the sun.

I love doing the splits,
Down and down I go,
One foot forward, one foot back,
I think it's really fun,
I practice in the sun.

I love doing headstands,
Up and up I go,
Hands on floor, toes in the air,
I think it's really fun,
I practice in the sun.

Summer holidays means it's time to play,
I go out in the garden and do them every day,
Splits, cartwheels and headstands,
I think it's really fun,
I practice in the sun.

Jade Adams (10)

My Favourite Things

Having a lie in on a Saturday, seeing my plant seed grow,
Settling down with a great book is my favourite thing you know.
Playing with my fluffy fat cat, and giggling with my mum,
And in the middle of the day, some ice cream
                         would do to fill my growling tum.

Dressing up and looking pretty, dancing all night long,
Having piggybacks from my dad, you know he's very strong,
Summer, winter, autumn and spring,
Think of all the presents Santa will bring.

Just in time to see my favourite TV show,
And out to the seaside we will soon go.
A dream of witches, unicorns and dragons,
Watching the elegant horses pull those heavy wagons.

Loads of new websites on the computer I will find.
Sleeping round my sister's house, they must be very kind.
Listening to music on my MP3,
Writing secrets in my diary, don't lose the key.

Kimberley Homer (11)

The Things I Like

I like to go on bike rides with my mum,
playing games and having fun.
PlayStation 2s are really great,
especially when you're with your mates.
Playing football in the park,
right up 'til it becomes dark.
Building Bionicles are the best,
but not as good as my DS.
But the things I like most of all,
are great holidays by the pool.

Callum Jordan (10)

A Poem About Me

Oh I do like a bit of coriander
On me pasta and on me lasagne
And if you were to say, ooh I don't want it that way
That's fine with me cos I'm no panda!

I like being a couch potato,
You don't have to do anything all day.
Just sit on the corner suite and watch the 50" screen
Do everything its way. Very neat!

And if you're a bit like me
Come and have a chat,
And we'll make *history*,
Sat upon a fur mat!

Paris Maddock Dickinson (11)

My Favourite Things

Doing art, watching TV
Getting my friends to play with me,
Going to the cinema, going in the pool
Going to theme park fun for us all!
Getting lots of jewellery when we go to town
Going to the circus and seeing the funny clown.
Listening to CDs on the radio
Going to London to see a show,
Playing on my Game Boy and on my PS2
And learning different things that I never knew.
Protecting the environment around my estate
Going to a summer fete,
Having a barbecue in the backyard
Playing games that are really hard.
Planting lovely flowers in the ground
And listening to a lovely sound,
Making up dance moves to a song
Dancing away all day long.
Playing with Tia, my brother's dog
And climbing on a great big log,
Going to bed late at night
Going to the park to fly a kite.
Sitting in the sun, going on my waterslide
I really, really love it when I'm outside.
Trying on clothes in a fashion show
And in winter playing in the snow.
Helping my mum cook the dinner
And eating healthy foods, so we all get thinner.
Going for a ride on my bike
Yes these are all the things I like.

Vicki Connelly (10)

My Local Beach

I love to go to my local beach,
One of my most favourite locations.
I love to sit there eating a peach,
One of my favourite formations.

I love to go bodyboarding,
When the waves are as big as whales.
I love to go snorkelling,
When the waves are as small as snails.

I love to go cycling,
When the tides are at their lowest.
I love to go swimming,
When the tides are at their highest.

I like it when there is lots of wind
And I can fly my kite,
But when there is too much wind to find,
There is far too much air to fight.

When there is barely any wind,
A little child comes out to play,
He runs around with a mind of his own
And picks up a bucket of sandy clay.

Sadly, due to the English weather,
It is only nice for a bit of the year,
One must no longer see the seagull's feather,
One must make it all seem better with a beer.

Harry Harvey Wood (11)

These Are My Hobbies And Favourite Things

Dancing and prancing and fun in the sun,
Going to bed when my long day is done,
Riding bikes, then playing queens and kings,
These are my hobbies and favourite things.

Birthdays and Easter and special times,
Apples and oranges, lemons and limes,
Reading a story or acting one out,
I also like to scream and shout.

Using rubbish to make things and then recycling after,
Going in the pool, TV and laughter,
Playing instruments like piano and clarinet,
Jumping and bouncing and playing with my pets.

Listening to music and silvery disco balls,
Emailing relatives and making long phone calls,
Playing pretend with all types of dolls,
Then relaxing and enjoying my summer hols.

Walking my dog along the beach sand,
Being happy and cheerful and to lend a hand,
Listening to birds tweet and sing,
These are my hobbies and favourite things.

Megan Wookey (9)

What I Like The Most!

A nimals like alligators as well as art too
B aking a cake and being with my mates
C ats that are cuddly and cute and me being cheeky too
D ecorating my doll house for the family to live in
E aster eggs and the Easter bunny
F un games at playtime and finding new friends
H aving a good time at home and school too
G etting presents on my birthday and Christmas
I ce cream that's ice-cold on a summer's day too
J umping on the trampolines and eating jelly
K ites that can fly into the universe and kitty cats too
L icking lollipops and licking icing off a spoon
M aking big splashes in a swimming pool in June
N oisily knocking on my door with my mate
              and making my parents come out
O pening presents on Christmas Day
P ulling string in a tug of war
Q uite frankly my favourite toy is Nintendo DS
R ightly so, I like many things
S inging and dancing all the time
T aking forever on the phone with my friends
U p and down the slide I go
V ariety of sweets for me to eat, in the kitchen cupboard
W atching TV, until my eyes turn square
X amount of toys scattered on my bedroom floor for me to play with
Y apping with my best friend
Z ebras at the zoo I like to see too.

Chloe Taylor (10)

So Much To Do, So Little Time

A cting has got to be first
B allet is definitely not the worst
C omputer games that drive me mad
D rawing pictures that make people glad
E ntertaining is surely cool
F ootball games we play at school
G rowing flowers to make the world bright
H ugging Mum and Dad at night
I magining I'm a star
J ourneys in my dad's car
K iwi is my favourite fruit
L aughing at jokes can be a hoot
M onkeying about is my cup of tea
N ice ice cream by the sea
O pening presents on my special day
P acking for holidays when we go away
Q uivering when the snow falls down
R abbits fluffy, black, white and brown
S ummertime when nights are light
T rampolining to a great height
U ltimate time spent with my friends
V isualising the latest trends
W obbly jelly on a plate
X mas Day is always great
Y o-yos spinning round and round
Z apping aliens never to be found.

So many favourite things, you see
Life is just so full of glee!

Annabel Bates (9)

My Favourite Things

A bee's sting,
A venomous thing,
As powerful as a golf club swing,
There's always a queen but never a king,
Upon tiptoes I look in trees,
Down on my knees, in search of bees.

Football is my favourite thing,
My number one player is Ledley King,
When he strides out on the right wing,
You'll see he's as fast as a bolt of lightning,
I think he should sign for Reading,
Because he's also brilliant at heading.

I love my mum, I love my dad,
They're always kind and never get mad
I love my brother Clarke,
I love his hair,
He's like my big warm teddy bear.

Brook Vaughan-Eason (10)

My Favourite Thing: Cheetahs

Elegant, dominant, stealthy,
A shadow,
What's that?
Prey!
A nip, a scratch, a bite, a kill,
To the lair I go,
Hungry shall the cubs be,
What is this?
They're gone!
The chase begins,
The scent of an unwelcome presence,
Baboons!
It approaches,
Tall above the long grass,
Yet keeping a low profile,
The cubs are nowhere to be seen,
Wait,
A squeak,
The final strand of hope,
Over there,
Lie the bodies of my children,
One survived,
Soaked in rain,
But safe,
A growl,
Sends the baboon running,
A nip shall put the cub in his place,
I am the queen of this land
My favourite thing's the cheetah.

Daniel Siddorn (11)

Here Are Some Of The Things I Like

Here are some of the things I like,
Maybe painting a picture or riding a bike.
Some of my favourite things take place in the sun,
Whenever I do them I always have fun.

Puppies, kittens and all fluffy things,
New clothes, make-up and sparkly earrings.
Staying up late on a Friday night,
Eating yummy chocolate and drinking fizzy Sprite.

I love to read my favourite books,
And go to the lake to feed the ducks.
Going to the beach and swimming in the sea,
Visiting the park and climbing a tree.

More of my favourite things are to sing and to dance,
And to watch wrestling when I get the chance.
Going outside to explore alone,
But my favourite thing of all is going back home.

Natalie Summerscales (11)

I Like . . .

I like playing games
Even when it rains.
I like watching telly
Even when I'm smelly!
I like stroking dogs
But not shifting logs.
I like washing my hair
Even for a dare.
I like reading books
Some about famous cooks.

Isabelle Smith (9)

My Favourite Things

These are a few of the things that I like . . .

Playing cricket, football too,
Picking blackberries, eating a few,
Making brownies, going to Guides,
Looking at stars in the starry skies.

Climbing trees, going to town,
Buying clothes with Dad's pounds,
Knitting scarves, reading books,
Gazing in mirrors, admiring my looks!

Eating fruit, smoothies and all,
These always make me grow so tall!
Drawing and arts and crafts,
Making people laugh and laugh.

Making animals out of plasticine,
Going to see films on the big screens,
These are a few of the things that I like,
Oh, I almost forgot . . .

        Riding my bike!

Antonia Dore (10)

My Favourite Things

I love my mum and my dad too
Especially when we go to the zoo
A picnic of lots of drink and food
I eat too much but it is really good
At home I play with my pet
But get really sad when he needs the vet
Bingo is my cat
He is fluffy and fat
My friends are good fun
We skip, play and run
Riding my bike
I can go as fast as I like
Shopping with Mum is really cool
Buying new clothes and things for school
Playing Nintendo and watching TV
'Animal Planet' and 'Crocodile Dundee'
I love to make sweets and bake
My favourite is chocolate cake
Painting pictures and making a mess
That's what I like to do best.

Kate Ramsay (10)

My Favourite Things

My favourite things are very simple.
It's not a skateboard or ball
In case I fall.
I like to play with pets
And I always do bets.
I like to go to the park
Because it's open till dark.
But best of all these things
I like to play on trampolines.
About my brothers,
I like to mess about with them.
I like to write stuff about them
Like one is the best
One is the worst
One is a pest
And one comes first.

Alexis Dasiukevich (9)

My Favourite Things

First is my trampoline
I bounce so high I can be seen
From the next street.
Second is my PlayStation 2
I can drive through streets
Or dance to the beats.
Third is my Lego
I've got boxes of it
I can build all day and not get bored of it.

Timothy Dasiukevich (11)

Untitled

My name is Katie, I love to smile
I like to go on my bike and cycle for a while
Downhill is easy, uphill is hard
By the time I finish my legs are bad.

I like to play my violin
Even though I make an awful din
A squeak and a squawk
My mother can't hear herself talk.
I like to play my Game Boy in the car
As we always travel very far
And those were a few of my favourite things.

Katie John (9)

Things That Make Me Happy

I like swimming,
Swimming is great,
I swam when I was 6, 7 and now I'm 8.

In the summer
Holidays are fun.
I like playing
In the sun.

But best of all I like Mum,
She makes me happy when I'm glum.

Annika Guru (8)

So I'd Like To Say I've Had A Good Day

My favourite thing
Is to sing,
Through the light
And through the night,
I also like
To ride my bike,
My heart is racing
While I am chasing,
Catching boys
With no noise,
I like to talk
But not to walk,
I do a cartwheel
And swim like a seal,
So I'd like to say
I've had a good day,
And I'll say goodbye
With a wink from the eye.

Sophie Garside (11)

My Favourite Things

M is for Mum, who cooks my tea.
Y is for yummy, such as sweets and ice cream.

F is for fun, playing out with my friends.
A is for animals, my hamster's fluffy and cute.
V is for violin, must practice every day.
O is for orange, the colour that I like.
U is for uncles, of which I have many.
R is for running, I'm running the Race For Life.
I is for Ireland, I've been there once before.
T is for tennis, Wimbledon here I come.
E is for elephants, part of Bolton town's heritage.

T is for TV, especially Tracy Beaker.
H is for holidays, with sun, sand and sea.
I is for Italian food, spaghetti Bolognese.
N is for night-time, when I get to sleep and dream.
G is for guitar, I go to guitar club after school.
S is for singing, watch out Britney Spears here I come.
These are a few of my favourite things.

Chloe Pendlebury (11)

The Best Things

I have lots of favourite things like going to the park
And playing on the swings.

I like to ride my bike
Looking at the sights.

Holding my brother, pretending I'm his mother
Doing my hair and going to the funfair.

Laughing at my dad when he's going mad
Watching movies and being groovy.

Dancing and singing never stops
While listening and rapping along to hip hop.

Going to school doing history and art.
One of my favourite things to paint are definitely love hearts.

Playing my PSP and watching TV
They're my favourite things, yeah!

Shyanne Duffus (10)

My Best Friend

M y best friend's name is Stacey
Y ou are the best!

B ecause we have known each other
E very day in our life
S tacey and me, best friends forever
T antrums will never come between us

F ooling about in our summer days
R iding our bikes together
I nventing at games
E njoying each other's company
N ever-ending friendship
D reaming of life in a sunny climate.

Hollie Smith (11)

My Favourite Things

Going to school
Because my teacher is so cool
Playing in the sun
With no homework to be done
Playing with my best friends
And driving my bike around big bends
Going to the shop
To buy my favourite Belfast bap.
Getting new clothes
Because I love to pose
I love to dance
And I do it every time I get a chance
Music is a great thing
I love to hear it and I love to sing
My favourite colour is anything pink
For another colour I would have to think
I love to dress up at Hallowe'en
Put on something scary and watch the young ones scream
Christmas is the best
You open all your presents and make loads of mess.

Maria Tomaszko (9)

All About Me - Katie B

I love trips, I eat crisps,
I love my age, I act on the stage,
I love to have dinner out, shout and jump about,
I like to sing in my favourite season spring,
I like to watch Tracy B but my mum doesn't let me,
I like to run, it's lots of fun,
I like to skip and after I have a kip,
I like to jump in the pool - pose, real cool!

Katie Boekestein (7)

Best Things

A hug from my mum
A kiss from my dad
Dressing up as a doctor
Or a queen being mad.

Playing with friends
Playing with family
Making fun stuff
It only depends.

Laptops and gadgets
And catching fish in a net
Playing football and netball
But best of all I have a pet.

Easter, Hallowe'en and Christmas
Eating chocolate, watching telly
Finding out mysteries
And sweets, treats in my belly.

'Top of the Pops' and reading a book
Doing something cheeky
Then let off the hook
Seeing things and able to look.

PlayStation and games
Barbies and robots
Puppies and string
And also learning about queens and kings.

Lauren Vine (10)

I Love Being . . . Me!

Oh I love candy and I love sweets,
Oh I love presents and I love treats,
Oh I love swimming with the dolphins in the sea,
I love being . . . *me!*

Oh I love playing on sunny days,
Oh I love performing in school plays,
Oh I love sipping honey and vanilla tea,
I love being . . . *me!*

Oh I love colouring with my new pens,
Oh I love getting 10 out of 10,
Oh I love going with my family on shopping sprees,
I love being . . . *me!*

Oh I love makeovers with sweet perfume,
Oh I love dressing up in fancy plumes,
Oh I love breaded fish with salty chips and peas,
I love being . . . *me!*

Oh I love praying and I love God,
I love Nintendo but not iPod,
Oh I love speaking in Urdu and Punjabi,
I love being . . . *me!* Oh yeah!

Qudsiyah-Bano Agha-Shah (9)

My Favourite Things

I like playing on laptops
I like 'Top of the Pops'
I like watching TV
I like a hug from my mummy
I like playing in the sun
I just love having fun
I like to ride my bike
I like to hike
I like bird catching
I like words matching
I like eating ice cream and sweets
I like queens and treats
I like playing with pets
I like scoring goals in the back of nets
I like reading books
I like doing things cheeky then getting off the hooks
I like to sing
I like to wear a ring
I like to swim
I like to play with Tim
I like to play
I do it all day
I like a clock
It goes tick-tock
I like snow
Sometimes I don't know where to go
I like the rain
It falls on a choo-choo train
I like puppets and strings
I like hanging on rings.

Angel Panford (7)

A Few Of My Favourite Things

Going on a journey there's different things to see
Hearing the birds and bees that is totally me!
Studying God-given nature all around
In the garden crawling on the ground
Pouring your imagination onto a white sheet
Be careful this has to be neat
Opening presents with people you love
As you know God is watching from above
Putting your head into an interesting book
It grips you like a fish on a hook
Feeling the beat as the music plays
It makes your body tingle in mysterious ways
Testing your brain
Splashing in puddles of rain
Watching an interesting movie
Maybe it is scary, romantic or groovy
Eating chocolate, ice cream and sweets
On your birthday opening treats
Stroking the fur of a cat or dog
Or even going on a healthy jog
Feeling the wind as you run on sports day
Reaching the finish line the crowd shouts hooray!
Winning a game you're the moon
Celebrate your best friend's birthday in June
Feeling warm when you get a hug
You feel like a cosy bed bug
Snuggling down into bed
Sweet dreams as you rest your head
Going to school and learning about kings
These are a few of my favourite things!

Anisa Howell (11)

My Favourite Thing

My mum is my favourite thing,
My mum is my valley,
My mum is my one true love
And my one true strength.

My mum is cunning,
My mum is smart,
I love my mum,
She's always kind and loving.

When I look into her face
She blossoms like a rose,
When I look into her eyes
They sparkle like diamonds,
She's my one and only love
That's why she's my mum.

Bopski Mbadiwe (8)

My Favourite Things

Listening to my favourite song.
Watching the film 'King Kong'.
Going to school
When the weather is cool.
Going to parties
As well as eating Smarties.
Playing on swings
Meeting the royal kings
These are my favourite things.

Tehreem Sehar (10)

My Favourite Things

Playing around and messing about
Having free time to scream and shout
Going on holiday on the plane
Going to countries as hot as Spain.

Going shopping with my friends
Being lazy on the weekends
Watching Beyoncé on TV
Going to Brighton to sit by the sea.

Listening to music and dancing around
Staying at home where it's safe and sound
Spending time with my mum and dad
Watching movies that make me feel sad.

Going to school to learn new things
Going to Claire's Accessories to get bracelets and rings
Going to Chessington or Thorpe Park
Going to my friend's house to hear her dog bark.

Turning almost a teenager and having a party
Going outside to paint and be arty
Eating ice cream on a hot summer's day
Going to the park with lots to do and play.

If I have things that I like to do
Such as having a party or visiting the zoo
Screaming whenever I watch my favourite singers sing
Then I think you also have favourite things.

Zainab Darong (12)

My Favourite Things

I like animals
And the book about Flanimals
I like making kites
And I love Chinese lights.
I also like dogs
And inventing with cogs
I like to surf
And run on a baseball turf.
I love the rain
And don't enjoy pain
I like lizards
And enjoy freezing cold blizzards.
I also like bees
And love swimming in seas
I like birds
And like zebras who run in herds.
I do like the colour green
And I don't like people who are mean
I enjoy books
And like extremely good cooks.
I also like mice
And like brown rice
I like puzzles
And feel sorry for dogs with muzzles.
I like to count money
And I like fresh bee honey
I like pop bands
And I like exploring forgotten lands
I wish I had wings
So I could write about them in my favourite things.

Dylan Van Lengen (9)

My Favourite Things

Chilling with my family, catching with my mate
Cruising down town with a hot chocolate shake
These are a few of my favourite things.

Going to the funfair, going to tall rides
Whizzing up, down, left, right, all around
These are a few of my favourite things.

Cooking and eating, chopping to making
Things out of leftovers or freshly cooked stew
These are a few of my favourite things.

Swinging on a swing, high, high, high
Until I can reach the blue sky
And fly with the birds free.

These are a few of my favourite things.

Shazia Tahir (11)

My Favourite Things

I like acting and dancing and playing
Pop Idol
Going to school and how to recycle
Diamonds and rubies and sapphire rings
Those are few of my favourite things.

I like clothes shopping and going to McDonald's
Watching some TV and getting into trouble
Causing mischief and playing on swings
Those are a few of my favourite things.

Playing with my brothers, Rashaan and Jaden,
I especially love it when they're behaving
Pretending to be a queen or a king
Those are a few of my favourite things.

Listening to music all day, going out to play
Rock and roll and pop, listening to it non-stop
I really like to sing
Those are a few of my favourite things.

I don't need to change, my life is great
Especially when I am on the estate
However the best thing in the world is being me
Those are a few of my favourite things.

Doing Young Writers and winning a prize
That should be a lovely surprise
Now I have finished what I have to do
But are these your favourite things too?

Rianna Dathorne (11)

My Favourite Things In Life

Day to day, what are my favourite things?
Well, it includes watching my best bands and singers,
Especially the love of my life, Shayne Ward.
Even when I hear or see Girls Aloud it makes me smile.
Going to watch Aston Villa play,
It turns into a better day.
At Christmas I love munching chocolate
And opening presents.
My birthday three days later,
More, more, more presents.
Going to concerts at the NEC,
Artists such as Westlife and the X Factor.
I love playing with my three-year-old nephew,
He always makes me smile.
My hobbies are singing, dancing and badminton,
Which I play a lot at school,
I enjoy searching on the Internet in ICT,
I'm very good in ICT and I really enjoy solving problems,
Although I'm not a big fan of school,
I love socialising with others.
So here was just some of my favourite things.

Michelle Bailey (15)

My Favourite Things In Life

My favourite things in life are
Going for a spin in my dad's car.
Going to the beach with my dog,
Running through a big bog,
Hiding behind a huge log.

My favourite things in life are
Eating a tasty chocolate bar.
Going on holiday to Whitley Bay
Playing outside on a nice day.

My favourite things in life are
Going in my friend's big car.
Cycling round the castle grounds,
Hearing all the nice sounds.

Well that's some of my favourite things,
I also like playing a game called Queens and Kings.

Lucy Macleod

My Favourite Things

My favourite things are big cuddles,
Fussing my cat and fussing my dog.

My favourite things are sunbathing, jumping in puddles
And playing in my garden.

My favourite things are relaxing,
Having a bath and pampering myself.

My favourite things are playing football,
Badminton and benchball.

My favourite things are sewing,
Doing my hair and listening to music.

My favourite things are playing cards,
Playing the keyboard and also Beehive Bedlam.

My favourite things are drawing,
Reading and writing.

My favourite things are Fray Bentos pies,
Brussels sprouts and roast dinners.

My favourite things are going on roller coasters,
Watching TV and playing my guitar!

These are my favourite things!

Amy Robinson (11)

This Is What I Like . . .

Animals and cars,
That's what I like,
Spending time with my family,
Or going out on my bike.
In the country,
Or downtown,
Going out and dressing up,
In my favourite gown.

Doing something exciting,
That's what I love,
Going on magic holidays,
Or something special sent from above.
Going motor racing,
Or on a shopping spree,
Chilling out with my friends
And going to the rugby.

My pets and relatives,
That's what I adore,
Going to a reunion,
Family galore.
Helping my mum out,
Looking after someone's little tike,
Making the best of life,
This is what I like.

Charlie Emsley (13)

My Favourite Things

Chocolate and candy
Feeling just dandy
Presents and parties
Lots of fun!

Tennis and basketball
Inside the city hall
Sitting out in the sun
Everyone!

Doggies and pussycats
Balls and baseball bats
These are a few
Of *my favourite things!*

William Carey (9)

I Like . . .

I like reading my book
I like watching my mum cook.
I really like sweets
I like presents, surprises and treats.
I like my younger brother
I like my sister and my mother.
I like the stars and moon
I like my birthday, coming soon!
I like Britney Spears
I like walking on piers.
I like coming home from school
I like going to the swimming pool.
I like dresses and shoes
I like hearing interesting news.
I like necklaces and hairbands
I like playing in bandstands.
I like wearing my ring
I like looking totally bling!
I like twisty slides
I like water rides.
I like playing with balls
I like shopping in malls.
I like a holiday
I like Christmas Day.
I like the colour blue
I like the colour pink too.
I like dolls and shows
I like the wind that blows.
I like queens and a king
But my favourite thing is to act, dance and sing.

Heleana Neil (10)

The Best Time

Reading and writing
Verily no fighting
Playing with mates
Not washing plates
Swimming in a pool
Hopefully not being a tool
Going shopping
Instead of chopping
Kicking a football
Not cleaning a hall
Telling a story
Not being able to feel glory
Putting make-up on
Indoubtably not being a con
Seeing the bright sun
Unfortunately not having fun
Cracking jokes
Maybe see the folks
What's fun and what's not?

Sapphire Walker (13)

Things I Like And Don't Like

I absolutely love swimming
But I don't like singing at all
I absolutely, positively hate spiders
Or any creepy-crawly.
When I'm down my friends and family come to me.

I would never ever eat peas
And I have a thing about keys.
Some days at school are very boring
But when I get home I love jumping in the pool.

So I hate singing, spiders,
Creepy-crawlies, peas and boring days at school
But I love swimming,
My friends and family coming to me when I'm down,
Keys and jumping in the pool
After a boring day at school.

Sian O'Loughlin (10)

My Toys

My toys are fun
But my number one toy
Is the best one
To play with in the sun
It's a water gun
And a water bomb
It's so much fun
To play with in the sun.
Where have my socks gone?

Dominic Hughes (8)

My Favourite Things

Things, things, my favourite things,
My favourite things,
Playing in bright sunshine,
Eating ice cream in hot summertime,
Going to school in bright sunlight,
In bright sunlight,
These are the few of my favourite things,
My favourite things,
Cooking things, visiting friends, sewing things,
Sewing things,
These are a few of my favourite things,
My favourite things,
Reading, listening and watching interesting, exciting things,
Laughing, smiling and giggling at funny things,
On funny things,
These are a few of my favourite things,
My favourite things,
Playing with teddies and sleeping with them,
Playing with babies and having a good time with them,
Having a good time with them,
These are a few of my favourite things,
My favourite things,
Things, things, my favourite things,
My favourite things.

Siddrah Shahid (14)

To Have It All

Skipping ropes, hopscotch
Leaf diving in fall
These are the things
To have it all
Camping, holidays
Swimming in the sun
Checking out a horror book
Or with friends, just having fun
Music that rocks
Writing poems for you
These are some things
To name just a few
Climbing trees
Scaling walls
In the garden
Or at the mall
CDs and albums
DVDs and games
'X Factor' and 'Pop Idol'
Just for the fame!
Soaps and movies
Gripping but fun
'Harry Potter', 'Stormbreaker'
Plus 'Chicken Run'
These are the best
Just to name a few
But there's one other thing . . .
And that's writing to you!

Natalie Steinmetz (12)

My Cat Jessie

My cat Jessie
Jess for short
She's silver all over
Just like shiny crystals
She's soft as a pearl
Her hair is curled
And don't forget that she's a girl
She purrs when you touch her fur
This shows that we love her forever
And that's my cat Jessie.

Amy Hodgkin (9)

Liverpool

Liverpool is my city
All the people are so witty
Liverbird is our guard
Looking for bad people to put behind bars
LFC are great, they're the best
Better than Everton, Chelsea and the rest
Walking around when it's hot
Going shopping for a new top
How about a drink in our posh pubs
Or maybe a dance in our amazing clubs
With our flashing lights and the drinks
And the smell of perfume or Lynx
Merseyside long and wide
We keep it clean to keep our pride
Radio City stands so tall
Stuck to St John's shopping mall
I love my city with all my mates
That's why we're capital of culture *in 2008.*

Melissa Manrow (10)

The Flower Hammock

When I look up at the sky blue
I see something amazing
Then I ask myself who
I look more closely
See that it's swinging
And if you have good eyesight
You will see it's a flower hammock
Swinging closer through the sky
Magical.

Sophie Meyer (8)

Are These Any Of My Favourite Things?

Playing football and going to school,
Swimming in the sea or in the swimming pool.
Sunbathing in the garden and playing on the swings,
These are some of my favourite things.

Playing on the computer and watching Stevie G,
Drawing people with Mrs T!
Playing hoopla with coloured rings,
These are some of my favourite things.

Eating crisps and Cadbury's Flakes,
Helping my dad if something breaks.
Eating cake that Grandma brings,
These are some of my favourite things.

Going to a restaurant that is posh,
Listening to the song 'At The Car Wash'.
Going to a party and wearing earrings,
These are some of my favourite things.

Making snowmen in the snow,
Seeing my cousin's baby sister grow.
Going to the seaside and seeing the jellyfish that sting,
These are all of my favourite things.

Rachael Lyon (9)

Favourite Things

F luffy rabbits at the farm
A pples I give to horses from my palm
V iolins and clarinets playing all day
O nly it's just the clarinet I play.
U nderwater when I swim
R acing fast, I love to win.
I love to read a Roald Dahl book
T hen I let my brother have a look
E ating sweets and chocolate bars

T he one I choose is always Mars
H aving time to laugh and play
I n my nanny's house on Saturday
N anny's table I always lay
G randad is great, he always sings
S o these have been a few of my favourite things.

Hannah Shore (8)

My Favourite Things

Computer games and enjoying the sun
Making friends, karaoke, holidays and fun.
Taking long walks, sitting in the breeze
Are these a few of your favourite things?

Birthdays and Christmas - present time for me!
Playing with friends, joking and laughing as we eat.
Going to school, learning about different things
Are these a few of your favourite things?

Watching TV, eating ice cream and sweets
Going to the movies - now that's a treat!
Dressing up and having fun
Are these a few of your favourite things?

Computers and mobiles and playing with your friends
Picnics in the park, the fun never ends!
Bike rides and walks in the bright sun
Are these a few of your favourite things?

Disney Channel and enjoying a good book
Rice Krispie cakes and fun to cook.
Singing to The Pussycat Dolls or Westlife
These are my favourite things.

Atlanta Repetti (10)

A Horse

A horse it has such pride
And always someone gets a ride
Sometimes big and sometimes small
Sometimes short and sometimes tall
Sometimes sleeping, sometimes leaping
Sometimes it could be racing
Otherwise it could be pacing
In a race its feet keep clicking
While the clock keeps on ticking
A horse it keeps on going fast
While the time goes right past.

Eve Richardson-Baldwin (9)

Mine All Mine

Chocolate bars
Convertible cars
And eating loads of sweets
Strawberry picking
Tasty chicken
And having lots of treats
Making dens
Felt-tip pens
And pink Converse boots
A plasma TV
An ice lolly
And when David Beckham shoots
Doing art
Pretty flowers
Shopping for several hours
Playing on swings
Diamond rings
Those are a few of my favourite things.

Danielle Elizabeth Bono Davies (11)